THE OFFICIAL ANNUAL 2012

A Grange Publication

Written by Michael Bridge

Designed by Colin Heggie

ISBN: 978-1-908221-37-7

£7.99

Contents

WELCOME

Dear Supporters

Welcome to the 2012 Official Tottenham Hotspur Annual.

My third season at the club was one of my most exciting in management. We loved every minute of our UEFA Champions League adventure. To say we were disappointed to lose to Real Madrid in the Quarter-Final shows how far we have come in such a short space of time.

We all wanted to finish in that fourth spot again but ultimately we fell short as we couldn't turn the draws into victories. If we couldn't get the fourth spot I wanted to finish fifth and we achieved that with victory at Liverpool and a home win over Birmingham. The top four is so difficult to break into but we've done it once and we're desperate to do it again.

Looking back on the season in depth, we've had some fantastic results which will live long in the memory. In the league we won at Arsenal for the first time since 1993 and did the double over Liverpool, when did Tottenham last achieve that? In Europe we made everyone sit-up and watch as we beat both Inter and AC Milan.

As I've said before, we're not too far off from achieving great things here. There isn't much that needs to change. At my previous clubs, I've always had to start from scratch but not here. We've got cover in most positions and with a bit of luck on the injury front I really believe we'll have a good season. However, nothing can be achieved without your support and we really do appreciate your loyalty at home and away.

I look forward to seeing you at the Lane for what I'm sure will be another exciting season.

THANKS AGAIN, COME ON YOU SPURS!

Harry Redknapp

UEFA Champions League Review

After finishing fourth in the previous season, UEFA Champions League football finally arrived at White Hart Lane. To say we took the competition by storm would be an understatement. The likes of Gareth Bale, Luka Modric and Rafael van der Vaart flourished on Europe's biggest stage and our European adventure for 2010-11 will never be forgotten.

UEFA Champions League Play-Off Round 1st Leg

YOUNG BOYS 3-2 TOTTENHAM HOTSPUR

Roman Pavlyuchenko and Sebastien Bassong kept our UEFA Champions League dream alive after we found ourselves 3-0 down in the first leg of our play-off at Young Boys. Shell-shocked would be an understatement. For years Tottenham Hotspur have waited for UEFA Champions League football and it looked like we were about to fall at the very first hurdle. Thankfully our two crucial away goals kept the tie very much alive.

UEFA Champions League Play-Off Round 2nd Leg

TOTTENHAM HOTSPUR 4-0 YOUNG BOYS

The glory, glory nights returned after comprehensively beating Young Boys in the second leg to earn a place in the group stages. A Peter Crouch hat-trick and another from Jermain Defoe turned round a 3-2 first leg score to win 6-3 on aggregate.

WERDER BREMEN 2-2 TOTTENHAM HOTSPUR

We were drawn in a very difficult group as holders Inter Milan, Werder Bremen and Dutch Champions FC Twente formed Group A. Our first game away to Werder Bremen couldn't have started any better as a Petri Pasanen own goal and a Peter Crouch header saw us race into a 2-0 lead. A Hugo Almeida goal just before half-time gave Werder Bremen hope. In the second half the German side levelled through the impressive Marko Marin. A draw was the least we deserved but it set us up well on day one of the UEFA Champions League group stages.

TOTTENHAM HOTSPUR 4-1 FC TWENTE

A comprehensive victory over Dutch Champions FC Twente saw us level with Inter Milan on four points. Rafael van der Vaart had a penalty saved as we went in at half-time goalless. Early in the second half van der Vaart did get on the score sheet with a classy left-footed finish. Roman Pavlyuchenko scored from the penalty spot to make it 2-0 before van der Vaart was sent off for two bookings. Twente's Nacer Chadli reduced the deficit but another well-taken Pavlyuchenko penalty and another from Gareth Bale earned victory.

INTER MILAN 4-3 TOTTENHAM HOTSPUR

This game will not be forgotten in a hurry. Goals from Zanetti, two from Eto'o and another from Stankovic gave the holders a 4-0 half-time lead. Gomes was sent off on 11 minutes. At half time, the general consensus was just how many more goals will Inter score. Thankfully, Gareth Bale was in the form of his life, scoring the most impressive hat-trick you're ever likely to see. The Tottenham supporters, scattered all over the stadium, were in fine voice and applauded the 10 men off at the final whistle. A sensational match but at full time the entire footballing world were in awe of Gareth Bale.

TOTTENHAM HOTSPUR 3-1 INTER MILAN

One of the all-time great European nights in our history. UEFA Champions League holders Inter Milan defeated at the Lane after a magnificent performance. And it was Gareth Bale once again who stole the show. Rafael van der Vaart opened the scoring and that was enough to give us a half-time lead. We extended the lead on 61 minutes, Bale again terrorising Brazilian full-back Maicon, crossed for Peter Crouch to finish. Samuel Eto'o scored with 10 minutes remaining but it was Bale again flying down the wing this time crossing for Pavlyuchenko to ensure a famous victory and put us on course for qualification into the knockout stages. White Hart Lane was rocking, Bale producing another world class performance, Modric masterful in midfield and Gallas the rock at the back. A wonderful night, the giant, that is Tottenham Hotspur, was wide awake once more!

TOTTENHAM HOTSPUR 3-0 WERDER BREMEN

Qualification to the knockout stages was guaranteed with a comfortable win over Werder Bremen. Luka Modric was the stand-out performer in this match, oozing class in central midfield. Modric scored our second of the game with a composed volley, after Younes Kaboul's header put us in front. Peter Crouch scored a late third to put the game beyond doubt.

FC TWENTE 3-3 TOTTENHAM HOTSPUR

Despite qualification being already achieved, Harry Redknapp was determined to win Group A and a draw in the Netherlands made sure we progressed as group winners. In an amazing game we took the lead after FC Twente goalkeeper Boschker miss-kicked the ball which trickled into the net. They levelled from the penalty spot through Danny Landzaat. Jermain Defoe restored our lead on 47 minutes before Twente levelled again through Rosales. Defoe scored again to make it 3-2 but a free-kick from Chadli earned a draw for FC Twente. We could now look forward to the last 16 draw in Nyon.

Group A - Final Table

	P	W	D	L	F	A	GD	PTS
1 Tottenham Hotspur (Q)	**6**	**3**	**2**	**1**	**18**	**11**	**7**	**11**
2 Inter Milan (Q)	6	3	1	2	12	11	1	10
3 FC Twente	6	1	3	2	9	11	-2	6
4 Werder Bremen	6	1	2	3	6	12	-6	5

UEFA Champions League Round of 16, 1st Leg

AC MILAN 0-1 TOTTENHAM HOTSPUR

Peter Crouch was the man once again to score the winner on another momentous night in the Club's history. When you win your group you expect to avoid the biggest guns in Europe. However, AC Milan were drawn to face Tottenham in the last 16, which was arguably the toughest second-placed opponent we could have been drawn against. But a brave and gutsy performance saw us take a priceless 1-0 lead back to White Hart Lane. Crouch was the hero at the City of Manchester Stadium on the night we qualified for the UEFA Champions League and now he put us in with a great chance of a place in the Quarter-Final. Aaron Lennon deserves credit for his great run into Milan's half, then perfectly placing the ball to Crouch to score. Without the influential Gareth Bale and Luka Modric a new star was born in the San Siro. Sandro was outstanding from start to finish, keeping the likes of Gattuso and Seedorf quiet. A huge job was complete in the San Siro but we knew we had to stay focused in the second leg.

UEFA Champions League Round of 16, 2nd Leg

TOTTENHAM HOTSPUR 0-0 AC MILAN

The Italian job was complete as AC Milan failed to break us down in the second leg at White Hart Lane. Peter Crouch's golden goal and that wonderful performance in the first leg at the San Siro, proved enough to topple the Italian giants and 2011 Serie A Champions. It was a change of focus in this second leg, as resolute defending all over the field was the aim, as opposed to our normal attacking endeavour in the European campaign. The UEFA Champions League dream continued and our victory in the first leg meant we were in the last eight.

UEFA Champions League Quarter-Final, First Leg

REAL MADRID 4-0 TOTTENHAM HOTSPUR

It was the dream draw. One of the biggest clubs in world football. This is what the UEFA Champions League is all about. After our superb form throughout the tournament, there was genuine hope we could get a result over two legs against Jose Mourinho's side. Sadly, our UEFA Champions league dream was all but over in the first leg, as an early Peter Crouch red card ruined what would surely have been a memorable match. Emmanuel scored twice, Angel Di Maria scored a cracking third and Cristiano Ronaldo all but killed our faint hopes with a soft fourth. Playing one of the greatest teams in world football with 11 men is hard enough, 10 men is impossible and so it proved.

UEFA Champions League Quarter-Final, Second Leg

TOTTENHAM HOTSPUR 0-1 REAL MADRID

Our European adventure officially came to an end as Cristiano Ronaldo's speculative 25-yarder squirmed through the grasp of Heurelho Gomes and bobbled agonisingly over the line for a 1-0 defeat on the night, 5-0 on aggregate. Jose Mourinho played his strongest available side despite having key games in the league and cup against Barcelona. The players gave everything but in truth, Real Madrid were very impressive. Despite the disappointment, we can look back on our wonderful European campaign.

Tottenham in the UEFA Champions League

18 We scored more goals than any other team in the group stages, four more than eventual winners Barcelona

1.9 The average goals per game we scored

5 Assists made by Aaron Lennon

7 Goals scored by Peter Crouch (Including play-off round)

Investec
Investec

Investec

Investec
Ford

Premier League Review

The 2010/2011 campaign created great excitement for all Spurs fans. Despite missing out on fourth place and another season of UEFA Champions League football, we achieved results that will live long in the memory of all Spurs fans. We recorded a rare victory at Anfield and our amazing 3-2 win over our rivals Arsenal at the Emirates Stadium. Juggling our UEFA Champions League adventure along with the rigours of Premier league football, saw us drop vital points in the race for the top four. Rafael van der Vaart arrived on transfer deadline day and became an instant hit with the supporters. Gareth Bale won the PFA Player of the Year award and we also saw the continued influence of Tom Huddlestone and Benoit Assou-Ekotto in the side, not forgetting the emergence of Sandro.

AUGUST

PLD: 3 W: 1 D: 1 L: 1
END OF MONTH POSITION: 11TH

Just months after beating them to fourth place the computer paired us with Manchester City for our first game of the season. In a match we dominated, visiting goalkeeper Joe Hart was all that stood between us and the goal on numerous occasions. Gareth Bale's stunning effort hit the inside of the post and somehow stayed out. A frustrating afternoon, but the players couldn't have done any more, as a stubborn City side held on for a point.

Seven days later we travelled to Stoke with only one fit striker in Peter Crouch. Despite our injury problems a double from Gareth Bale, one a goal of the season contender, saw us clinch an impressive 2-1 victory. You could even witness some of the home supporters applauding the goal.

Just three days after clinching a place in the UEFA Champions League group stages Wigan brought us back down to earth with a shock 1-0 win at White Hart Lane. Like Manchester City on the first day, we saw another heroic goalkeeping performance as Ali Al Habsi frustrated us all afternoon.

SEPTEMBER

PLD: 3 W: 1 D: 1 L: 1
END OF MONTH POSITION: 8TH

Our trip to West Brom saw William Gallas and Rafael van der Vaart make their Tottenham debuts. Luka Modric put us in front on 27 minutes before Chris Brunt levelled to earn a point for the home side.

Last season Wolves claimed a surprise double over us and it looked like Mick McCarthy's men were going to earn another victory at White Hart Lane. But late goals from Rafael van der Vaart, Roman Pavlyuchenko and Alan Hutton saw us secure all three points.

We suffered a disappointing 1-0 defeat away to West Ham in the final league game of the month.

OCTOBER

PLD: 4 W: 2 D: 1 L: 1
END OF MONTH POSITION: 6TH

Two goals from Rafael van der Vaart were enough to defeat Aston Villa in an exciting match. After falling a goal behind van der Vaart's header just before half-time made it 1-1. His second goal was world class. A deft touch left Richard Dunne grounded and he followed that up with a fine finish.

Just a few days away from a trip to the San Siro, a league meeting at Fulham looked awkward but goals from Pavlyuchenko and Tom Huddlestone secured our first win at Craven Cottage for eight and a half years.

After our thrilling match against Inter Milan we were held to a 1-1 draw at home to Everton. Rafael van der Vaart's good form continued, levelling after Leighton Baines put Everton in front with an unstoppable free kick.

We ended the month with a trip to Old Trafford and, once again, it was a familiar story as a refereeing decision went against us as we went down 2-0, with goals from Nemanja Vidic and a highly controversial second from Nani.

NOVEMBER

PLD: 5 W: 3 D: 1 L: 1
END OF MONTH POSITION: 5TH

Our most exciting month of the season was in November. However it didn't start well, as we suffered a 4-2 defeat at Bolton.

Three days later we were held at home to Sunderland, van der Vaart once again on target.

We secured our first league win in five matches as we beat Blackburn 4-2. Two goals from Gareth Bale and further strikes from Roman Pavlyuchenko and Peter Crouch were enough to record victory.

Seven days later it was the North London Derby at the Emirates. Goals from Nasri and Chamakh put Arsenal 2-0 ahead at half time. A classy finish from Gareth Bale gave us hope. Soon after van der Vaart's penalty made it 2-2 and the unlikely comeback was complete after Younes Kaboul's header made it 3-2 to Spurs. An amazing victory and our best league win of the season.

We finished the month off with a 2-1 win over Liverpool. A great run by Luka Modric resulted in Martin Skrtel putting the ball into his own net. A stoppage time goal from Aaron Lennon earned another satisfying victory.

DECEMBER

PLD: 4 W: 2 D: 2 L: 0
END OF MONTH POSITION: 5TH

December started with a 1-1 draw away to Birmingham. Sebastien Bassong was on target for Spurs.

Champions Chelsea were up next in the league. Pavlyuchenko put us in front with a fine finish. Didier Drogba levelled for Chelsea. Heurelho Gomes also saved a Drogba penalty in stoppage time.

On Boxing Day we travelled to Villa Park in what was one of our most impressive performances of the season. Rafael van der Vaart opened the scoring before Jermain Defoe was harshly sent off. Despite being down to 10 men we went on to add a second. In one of the most well worked goals of the season, Gareth Bale ran nearly the entire length of the field finding Aaron Lennon who set-up van der Vaart for his second of the afternoon. Villa pulled a goal back, but we held on to earn victory.

Newcastle were at White Hart Lane two days later. Aaron Lennon opened the scoring and a late Bale goal sealed victory to round off a good Christmas period. We ended 2010 in fifth place and qualification to the last 16 of the UEFA Champions League.

JANUARY

PLD: 4 W: 1 D: 2 L: 1
END OF MONTH POSITION: 5TH

Our good form over Christmas continued with a 1-0 win over Fulham. Gareth Bale scored the only goal of the game.

Our 11 game unbeaten run came to an end against Everton at Goodison. Rafael van der Vaart was on target for us.

David Beckham spent nearly two months training with the club and he was an interested spectator as we drew 0-0 at home to his former club Manchester United.

Steven Pienaar made his Spurs debut in a 1-1 draw at Newcastle. Aaron Lennon scored a stoppage time equaliser.

FEBRUARY

PLD: 4 W: 3 D: 0 L: 1
END OF MONTH POSITION: 4TH

Peter Crouch's good goal scoring form against Blackburn continued as we beat Blackburn 1-0 at Ewood Park.

There was a thrilling beginning and end in our next match at home to Bolton. Rafael van der Vaart opened the scoring from the penalty spot. We were then awarded another penalty, which van der Vaart missed. A Daniel Sturridge goal made it 1-1 but a magnificent effort from Niko Kranjcar in stoppage time, sealed victory.

Kranjcar was the hero again in our next match as we beat Sunderland 2-1 at the Stadium of Light. Michael Dawson levelled after Asamoah Gyan put Steve Bruce's side in front.

After our amazing win over AC Milan we travelled to Blackpool knowing that victory would put us in third place. Despite dominating, we were frustrated by Ian Holloway's side and went down to a 3-1 defeat, Roman Pavlyuchenko on target for us in stoppage time.

MARCH

PLD: 2 W: 0 D: 2 L: 0
END OF MONTH POSITION: 5TH

Only two league games in March and two draws dented our chances of another fourth place finish. We travelled to Wolves, who were deep in relegation trouble. Before play got under way, there was an emotional tribute to former Wolves and Tottenham player Dean Richards, who died aged 36 after a long battle with illness. Kevin Doyle put Wolves in front before two outstanding goals from Jermain Defoe made it 2-1. Doyle's penalty levelled shortly before half time. Roman Pavlyuchenko's powerful strike made it 3-2 but Steven Fletcher's late goal meant we left with only a point from an exciting match.

In our only other league match of the month we found Robert Green in great form again as we were frustrated by the West Ham 'keeper. Gareth Bale, Luka Modric and Rafael van der Vaart were all denied, by wonder saves from Green.

APRIL

PLD: 5 W: 1 D: 3 L: 1
END OF MONTH POSITION: 5TH

We started a crucial month with a 0-0 draw against Wigan at the DW Stadium.

After a 4-0 defeat to Real Madrid in Spain we bounced back with a 3-2 win over Stoke. Peter Crouch scored two, while Luka Modric's great solo effort gave us a 3-2 half time lead and we held on in the second half to earn all three points.

After our UEFA Champions League exit, it was the North London Derby. Theo Walcott put Arsenal in front on five minutes, but Rafael van der Vaart levelled two minutes later. Samir Nasri restored Arsenal's lead before Robin van Persie made it 3-1 to Arsenal. Shortly before half-time a brilliant long range effort from Tom Huddlestone made it 3-2. A van der Vaart penalty in the second half gave us a deserved point.

We dropped two vital points in our next match against West Brom. Under Roy Hodgson, West Brom became a tough side to beat and they proved so at White Hart Lane as Peter Odemwingie put them in front. Roman Pavlyuchenko levelled in the first half and Jermain Defoe made it 2-1 on 66 minutes but on 81 minutes, Simon Cox scored a stunning equaliser to severely dent our UEFA Champions League hopes.

Our final game of the month was the highly controversial 2-1 defeat at Chelsea. Sandro opened the scoring with a stunning effort outside the area. The first controversial moment arrived shortly before half-time. Heurelho Gomes was unable to hold Frank Lampard's long-range effort, and with the ball rolling towards the net the goal was given, despite Gomes clearly stopping the entire ball crossing the line. Chelsea won the match with three minutes remaining as Salomon Kalou scored despite being in an offside position.

MAY

PLD: 4 W: 2 D: 1 L: 1
FINAL POSITION: 5TH

A home draw against Blackpool all but ended our hopes of UEFA Champions League football. Charlie Adam scored from the penalty spot for Blackpool. Jermain Defoe levelled late in the game but a point didn't help in our quest for another year at Europe's top table.

Similar to last season we would face a trip to Manchester City in a rearranged match. An unlucky deflection from Peter Crouch into his own net was enough to settle this match. The result

meant City were guaranteed UEFA Champions League football for the first time in their history.

There were two games remaining – next up, a trip to Liverpool. Goals from Rafa van der Vaart and Luka Modric secured a 2-0 scoreline and sealed a first victory at Anfield since August, 1993. It also meant we were back in 5th at the expense of Liverpool.

Our final game of the season was a home match against Birmingham City. In an exciting final day we were looking to secure fifth place while Birmingham were deep in relegation trouble. Roman Pavlyuchenko's superb finish from outside the area. Craig Gardner equalised for Birmingham. That goal looked to have kept Birmingham in the Premier League but Wigan scoring at Stoke, meant they had to win our match. With Alex McLeish throwing every player forward, they were short at the back and Pavlyuchenko scored another stunning effort to relegate Birmingham and seal fifth place for Spurs. And so, a memorable 2010-11 campaign ended on a fitting high note.

Whilst there is obvious disappointment we won't be in UEFA Champions League competition for a second successive year, it makes us even more determined for the season ahead.

Final Premier League Table

		HOME					AWAY						
	P	W	D	L	F	A	W	D	L	F	A	GD	PTS
1 Man Utd	38	18	1	0	49	12	5	10	4	29	25	+41	80
2 Chelsea	38	14	3	2	39	13	7	5	7	30	20	+36	71
3 Man City	38	13	4	2	34	12	8	4	7	26	21	+27	71
4 Arsenal	38	11	4	4	33	15	8	7	4	39	28	+29	68
5 Tottenham	**38**	**9**	**9**	**1**	**30**	**19**	**7**	**5**	**7**	**25**	**27**	**+9**	**62**
6 Liverpool	38	12	4	3	37	14	5	3	11	22	30	+15	58
7 Everton	38	9	7	3	31	23	4	8	7	20	22	+6	54
8 Fulham	38	8	7	4	30	23	3	9	7	19	20	+6	49
9 Aston Villa	38	8	7	4	26	19	4	5	10	22	40	-11	48
10 Sunderland	38	7	5	7	25	27	5	6	8	20	29	-11	47
11 West Brom	38	8	6	5	30	30	4	5	10	26	41	-15	47
12 Newcastle	38	6	8	5	41	27	5	5	9	15	30	-1	46
13 Stoke	38	10	4	5	31	18	3	3	13	15	30	-2	46
14 Bolton	38	10	5	4	34	24	2	5	12	18	32	-4	46
15 Blackburn	38	7	7	5	22	16	4	3	12	24	43	-13	43
16 Wigan	38	5	8	6	22	34	4	7	8	18	27	-21	42
17 Wolves	38	8	4	7	30	30	3	3	13	16	36	-20	40
18 Birmingham	38	6	8	5	19	22	2	7	10	18	36	-21	39
19 Blackpool	38	5	5	9	30	37	5	4	10	25	41	-23	39
20 West Ham	38	5	5	9	24	31	2	7	10	19	39	-27	33

Rafael van der Vaart

With just minutes remaining of the 2010 summer transfer window, Spurs secured the signing of Dutch International Rafael van der Vaart. The 28-year-old admits his first season could not have gone much better after his transfer from Real Madrid.

The Dutchman became an instant hit with supporters after scoring on his home debut against Wolves. 'Rafa' scored 15 goals in all competitions, and was nominated for the PFA Players' Player of the Year award. Reaching the UEFA Champions League Quarter-Finals was his particular highlight, and getting to fourth place was all that could have made the campaign sweeter.

Rafael came through the ranks at Ajax and won two league titles and a Dutch Super Cup during 141 appearances with the Eredivisie side, scoring 60 goals before leaving for Hamburg in the summer of 2005. He was the Bundesliga side's leading scorer in his first season in Germany and in total made 111 appearances for Hamburg and went on to captain the club, before joining Real Madrid ahead of the 2008/09 campaign. There he spent two seasons, making 71 appearances in total. Rafael has been capped over 80 times by his country since making his international debut against Andorra in 2001 at the age of 18. He has represented the Netherlands at two European Championships and two World Cups, including the 2010 Finals in South Africa.

After spells in Holland, Germany and Spain, Rafa brought vital experience to the Tottenham squad, with many of our players still yet to sample the thrill of UEFA Champions League football. It's not easy leaving a club like Real Madrid, but English football attracted Rafa and he is delighted with how the move has turned out. "The Premier League is the biggest in the world. Everybody in every country sees our games and that's a nice thing."

"As a player you want to show what you can do to the whole world, so it has been an important move for me."

"I couldn't have really imagined it would have gone as well as it did, I had a great season.

"You have your ups and downs, but at the end I scored 15 goals. The team played well and it was a great UEFA Champions League season."

Last season saw Rafa just playing off the main striker. His partnership with Peter Crouch proved to be very successful and it was a system that worked well in Europe. He endeared himself further to the Tottenham supporters with his penalty at Arsenal, plus a great equaliser in the derby at White Hart Lane. He also scored one of the goals of the season in May, when his dipping volley helped us earn a 2-0 win at Anfield. Once again, Rafa's versatility and experience will be crucial as we look to get back in the top four this season.

Investec
"As a player you want to show what you can do to the whole world"

Gareth Bale

TOTTENHAM HOTSPUR YOUNG PLAYER OF THE YEAR & PFA PLAYER OF THE YEAR

Gareth received the Club's Young Player of the Year award for the second successive season after a memorable campaign. Bale also won the very prestigious PFA Player of the Year Award. The Welsh International set the world alight with amazing performances in the League and in the UEFA Champions League.

Great things were expected of Gareth last season after his blistering form at the end of the 2009/10 campaign. He was outstanding in our first game of the season against Manchester City. A week later he scored two goals at Stoke, one a goal of the season contender with an unstoppable volley. Gareth scored 11 goals in 40 games last season but it was his form in the first half of the season that earned the rewards. In the second half of the campaign, Gareth suffered back and ankle injuries, which restricted his appearances from January onwards.

After such an amazing season, it's hard to pick out a particular stand -out performance, but many will point to his stunning hat-trick at the San Siro against Inter Milan. Trailing 4-0, it was hard to find any positives in a match which was turning out to be one to forget, until Bale took over. His first two goals were surging runs down the left wing. His third was another well-placed effort after good work from Aaron Lennon. Jermaine Jenas summed up Bale's performance perfectly. "He was brilliant, absolutely brilliant. I can't speak highly enough of the lad. He's made one of the best right-backs in the world look pretty average defensively." Some would argue his performance in the home match against Inter Milan was even better. Less than a fortnight after scoring a hat-trick at the San Siro, the Welsh wizard stole the show with an arguably even better display, to help us secure a famous 3-1 win against the European champions in Group A of the UEFA Champions League. His raids down the left flank, left highly-rated full-back Maicon - voted last season's best defender in the UEFA Champions League - in a spin. He tormented the Brazilian international all night and set-up our second and third goals in the second half. Many described it as an 'Incredi-Bale' performance. Other highlights include his spectacular volley against Stoke in the Premier League in August and kick-starting our comeback from 2-0 down to beat Arsenal 3-2 with our first goal at the Emirates. All these memorable moments saw Bale claim the PFA Player of the Year award. Gareth became the fourth Spurs player to lift the award following Pat Jennings in 1975-76, Clive Allen in 1986-87 and David Ginola in 1998-99.

Gareth is looking forward to an injury-free campaign, as we chase a UEFA Champions League spot in the Premier League. "It was a good first half to the season but a frustrating second half for myself. But aside from the injuries it was a good one all round and one I'm looking to build on."

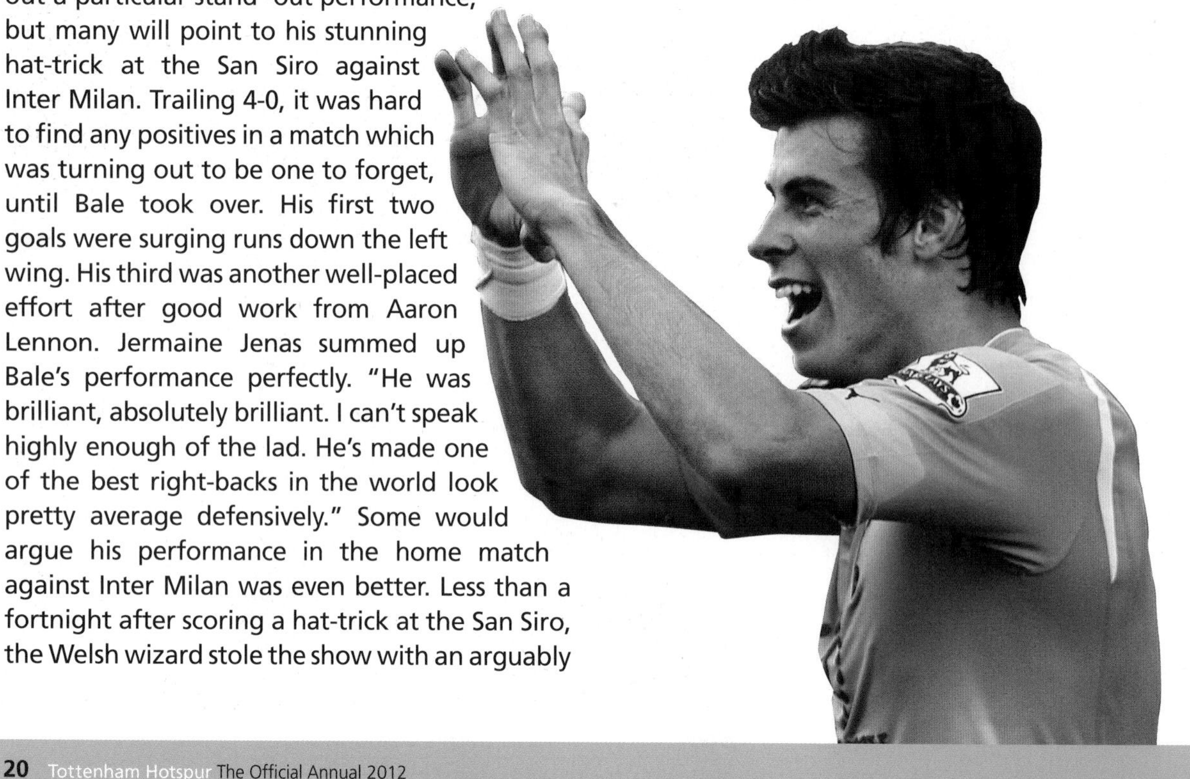

"It was a good first half to the season but a frustrating second half for myself"

Harry Redknapp

In his third season at Tottenham Hotspur, Harry Redknapp was in charge of a UEFA Champions League club for the first time in his career. Like the supporters, it's an experience he will never forget and he's hungry for more.

Our UEFA Champions League adventure was new to everyone including Harry. Juggling European football and the Premier League was never going to be easy, so it was no surprise Harry gave great credit to the players at the end of last season, for fighting off the challenge of Liverpool and finishing fifth. "We couldn't quite make the top four again, however, to have played in the UEFA Champions League, to reach the last eight in our first-ever year in the competition, was an amazing achievement and to finish fifth in the Premier League, the lads have done so well, they have been fantastic."

Naturally, Harry is disappointed we weren't able to compete at Europe's top table for a second successive year, but too many dropped points in the second half of the season meant a top four finish wasn't possible. "We obviously had a dodgy little run late on, where we were drawing too many games all of a sudden but we will give it another go this season."

Looking back on last season, we witnessed the return of the 'Glory, Glory Nights' at White Hart Lane, with victories over European Champions Inter Milan, Young Boys, FC Twente and Werder Bremen, not forgetting our amazing 1-0 victory against AC Milan in the San Siro. "There are so many great games and memorable nights - coming back from 3-0 down against Young Boys when it looked like we were going out in the qualifying stage of the UEFA Champions League, winning in Milan with Gareth Bale scoring a hat-trick against Inter Milan. "Beating the European champions, Inter at the Lane was a special night. We really ripped them to pieces, it was a great performance and I'll never forget the atmosphere."

Despite missing out on a place in the top four, our victory at Arsenal was arguably the highlight of the season. Our poor form at Anfield also ended as we beat Liverpool 2-0 in May. "Winning at The Emirates was a great day for the fans. I don't think anyone gave us a hope at half-time. The players believed we could get back into it, which we did, winning 3-2. It was a great feeling and it's games like these that make you love the job you do. Our win at Liverpool is right up there for me too, to go there and win, it's a rarity for Tottenham. Four wins in 99 years just shows you how difficult the club has found it to win there, but we did it and deserved it. It was a great performance."

Now in his 29th year as a Manager, Harry reveals his greatest thrill is still watching players train week in week out. "We have a terrific set of lads here. They're all fantastic players but they're good boys too. Picking a team is a tough job especially here with the talent we have. They always give me 100% and that's all I ask for."

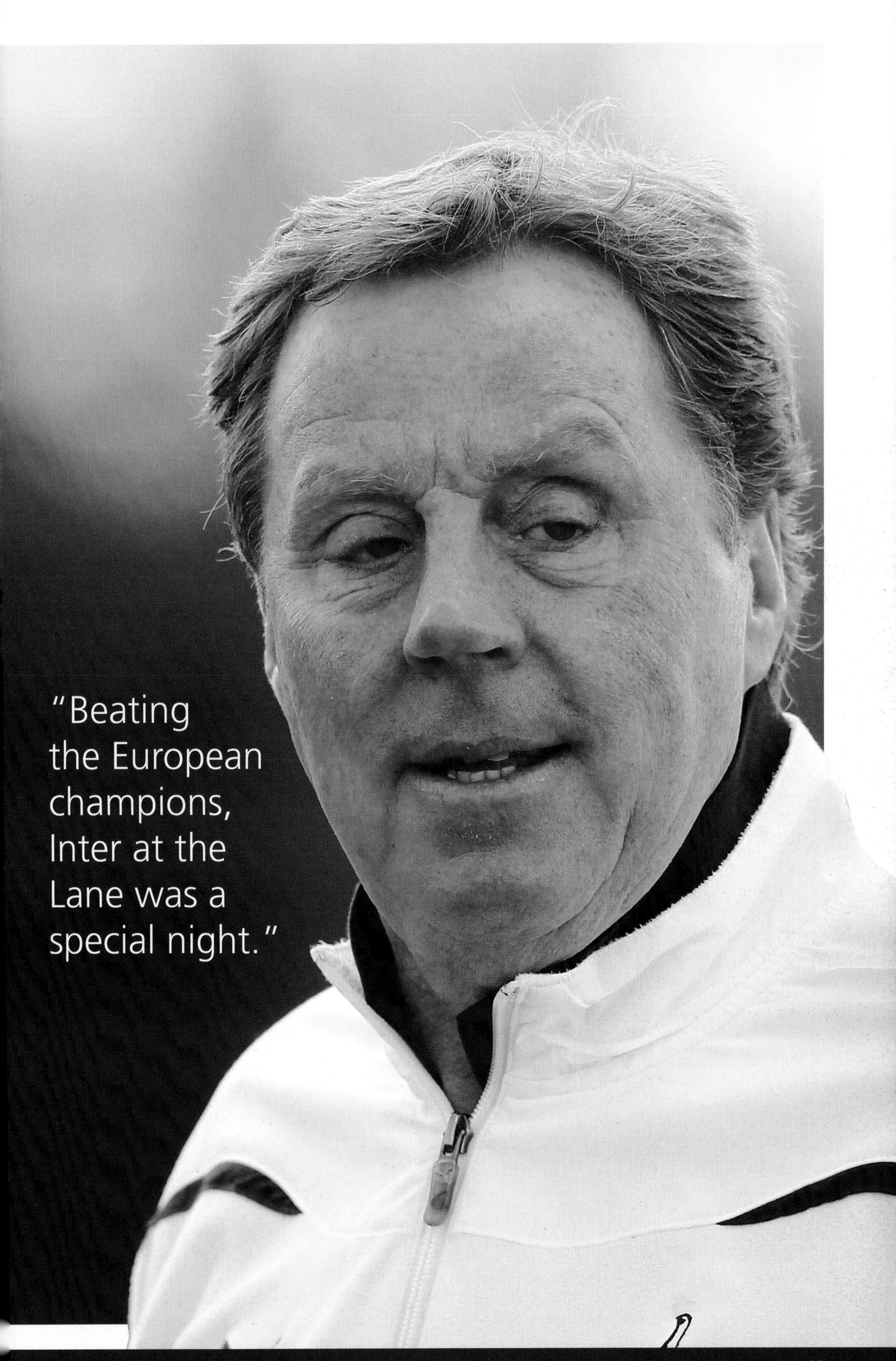
"Beating
the European
champions,
Inter at the
Lane was a
special night."

PLAYER **PROFILES**

2011/2012

Brad Friedel ▶

Brad joined Spurs in June 2011 after leaving Aston Villa at the end of his contract. The 40-year-old has spent the majority of his career at Blackburn Rovers and Aston Villa earning a reputation as one of the most consistent goalkeepers in the Premier League.

Carlo Cudicini ▲

Carlo joined Spurs from Chelsea in January 2009. He has provided strong competition for the number one jersey. He was in goal last season when we beat Inter Milan 3-1 at White Hart Lane. His impressive performances near the end of the season were enough to earn him a new one-year contract.

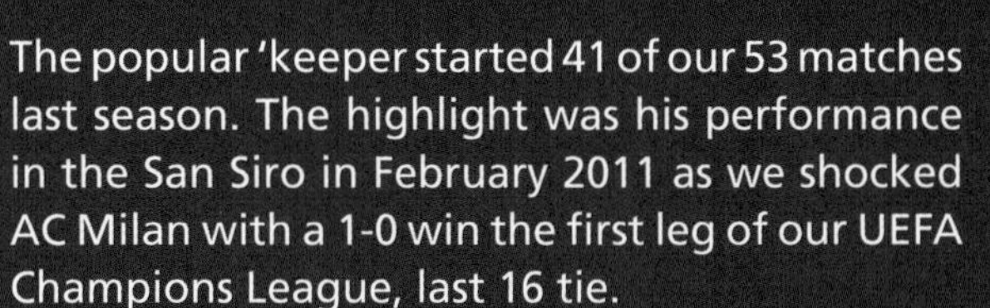

Heurelho Gomes ▼

The popular 'keeper started 41 of our 53 matches last season. The highlight was his performance in the San Siro in February 2011 as we shocked AC Milan with a 1-0 win the first leg of our UEFA Champions League, last 16 tie.

Gareth Bale ▶

The powerful left-sided Welsh international was voted PFA Player of the Year for 2011. Gareth's amazing performances in the UEFA Champions League have made him one of the most talked about players in world football. He scored an impressive 11 goals for the club last season. Gareth was also voted our Young Player of the Year last season.

Vedran Corluka ▲

Now in his fourth season at the club, 'Charlie' started the campaign in the right-back role but a combination of injury plus the form of Alan Hutton and Younes Kaboul restricted him to 24 appearances in all competitions in 2010-11. Vedran featured against AC Milan and Real Madrid last season.

Younes Kaboul ▼

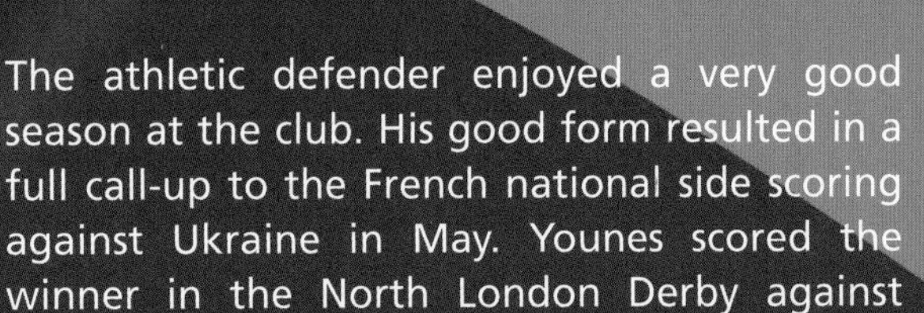

The athletic defender enjoyed a very good season at the club. His good form resulted in a full call-up to the French national side scoring against Ukraine in May. Younes scored the winner in the North London Derby against Arsenal last season.

Michael Dawson ▶

Popular, super-consistent central defender 'Daws' admitted 2010-11 was a season of incredible highs - and one, painful low. He suffered a serious ankle injury against Bulgaria in September but returned to play a key role in our UEFA Champions League campaign. Michael is our proud Team Captain.

Ledley King ▲

Injuries again took their toll on our Club Captain and longest-serving player in 2010-11. But Ledley's infamous knee wasn't the problem - this time, a groin injury restricted the classy central defender to nine starts out of 53. However, he did have the honour of leading us out for our first-ever UEFA Champions League match at the Lane - the second leg of the play-off against Young Boys in August - and ticked past the 300-appearance mark for the Club when he returned from a seven-month absence with an amazing performance in the 2-0 win at Liverpool in May.

Kyle Walker ▼

Young, flying full-back impressed in a loan spell in the Premier League at Villa in the second half of 2010-11. His performances secured a place in Stuart Pearce's squad for the European Under-21 Championships in Denmark in June, 2011 and he was a shining light despite England's early exit, starting all three group matches. He made his Spurs debut against Portsmouth in March, 2010.

Danny Rose

The young midfielder guaranteed his place in Spurs history with a stunning goal in the 2-1 win against Arsenal in April, 2010. After a loan spell at Bristol City last season Danny returned to Spurs and did a fine job a left-back near the end of the season.

William Gallas

The experienced French defender joined us on a one-year contract in August, 2010. Gallas joined on a free transfer after leaving Arsenal. William's consistency earned him a two-year extension on his contract, keeping him at the Club until 2013. In a masterstroke by Harry Redknapp, William captained the side in our 3-2 win over Arsenal at the Emirates last season and was voted Man of the Match with a superb performance.

Benoit Assou-Ekotto

Now a key member of the first team. Benoit is regarded as one of the top left-backs in the Premier League. Benoit played in 45 of our 53 matches last term. Indeed, he started 45 of our first 48 games before a late hamstring injury ruled him out for the last three weeks of the season and he was our only player to start all 12 matches in the UEFA Champions League.

Aaron Lennon ▲

Aaron featured in 46 matches for Spurs last season. The flying winger caught the eye in the UEFA Champions League and provided the crucial assist for Peter Crouch's goal against AC Milan in the San Siro. This is Aaron's seventh season at the club and the England international continues to play an important part in the side.

Tom Huddlestone 

The stylish midfielder captained the side when we beat Inter Milan 3-1 at White Hart Lane. A serious ankle injury restricted Tom to only 20 matches last season but there is no doubt when fit he is a key member of the first team. Tom has also been capped by England on three occasions.

Sandro

The Brazilian international is already a key member of the Spurs side. He joined the club in August after winning the Copa Libertadores with Internacional. He was sensational away to AC Milan in the UEFA Champions League and his great form continued for the rest of the season. He also scored one of the goals of the season against Chelsea in April.

Steven Pienaar

Steven joined Tottenham from Everton in January 2011. After beating off competition from Chelsea, Steven immediately settled into the side playing an important role in our 1-0 win at AC Milan. His work rate & versatility will be very important in another long campaign ahead.

Luka Modric

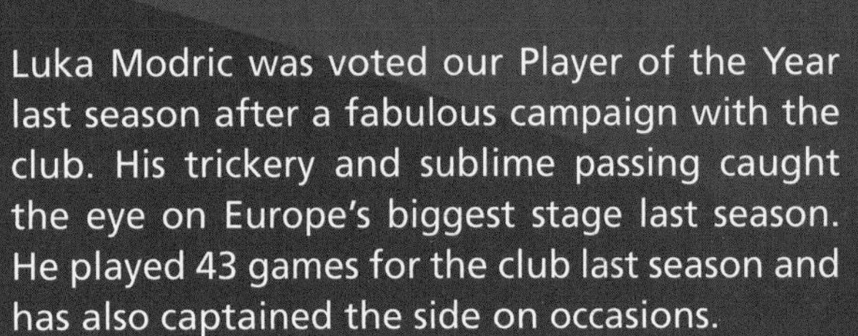

Luka Modric was voted our Player of the Year last season after a fabulous campaign with the club. His trickery and sublime passing caught the eye on Europe's biggest stage last season. He played 43 games for the club last season and has also captained the side on occasions.

Niko Kranjcar

The Croatian international found opportunities limited with the form of Gareth Bale but when he did feature he made an impact scoring the winning goal against Bolton in stoppage time and just a week later his cracking effort won the match at Sunderland.

Rafael van der Vaart

Rafael made a huge impact in his first season at the club. Our 2010 deadline day signing scored 14 goals in his first season in England. A crowd favourite, 'Rafa' further endeared himself to the White Hart Lane crowd with a goal against Arsenal in the 3-3 draw. He also scored the equaliser at the Emirates Stadium. The Netherlands international can play in central midfield, on the wing or just behind the striker which adds to his importance to the side. His partnership with Peter Crouch last season was successful especially in Europe.

Jermain Defoe 

Jermain had a mixed season with Tottenham after missing key games with an ankle injury suffered on England duty. He scored eight goals in 29 games last season. When fit Jermain is still one of the most feared strikers in the Premier League.

Roman Pavlyuchenko

The Russian International is a crowd favourite. He scored 13 goals last season including two fantastic strikes on the final day of the season against Birmingham. It's unfair to label the Russian as a 'super sub' but his impact coming off the bench usually resulted in a crucial goal for Spurs. He now aims to become our number one striker over the course of this season.

TOTTENHAM HOTSPUR 3
INTER MILAN 1
THE RETURN OF THE GLORY, GLORY NIGHTS

LENNON
7
CROUCH
15
8
SAMUEL
25
Investec
6
HUDDLESTONE
6
15

Derby Delight

We registered our first away win over North London rivals Arsenal for 17 years after a stunning comeback. Arsenal were on course to secure victory after leading 2-0 at half-time, but a second half revival earned a memorable win.

Arsenal deserved their lead, Samir Nasri opened the scoring on nine minutes. The home side continued to dominate and Marouane Chamakh's close-range finish put Arsenal in control.

Jermain Defoe replaced Aaron Lennon at half-time, as Manager Harry Redknapp looked to find a lifeline in a game which means so much to both sets of supporters. Defoe's introduction made an instant impact. The England striker flicked on a long ball from Benoit Assou-Ekotto and Rafael van der Vaart had the vision to play in Gareth Bale, who calmly slotted past Lukasz Fabianski.

The home crowd became anxious, we began to dominate. Luka Modric was impeded midway through the half and van der Vaart looked to curl his free-kick from 20-odd yards. For some reason, Fabregas threw his arm in the way of his shot and referee Mr Dowd pointed to the spot. Step up van der Vaart and his well-taken penalty meant we were on level terms.

After that there was only going to be one winner. Bale was causing the Arsenal defence all sorts of problems and was crudely chopped down on two occasions in the closing stages. From the second one a van der Vaart swinging free-kick into the area was glanced into the back of the net by Younes Kaboul. The five minutes of stoppage time felt like another 90, but when the final whistle went, the away end erupted. Arsenal were stunned as we completed an astonishing comeback.

Rafael van der Vaart was superb in both matches against Arsenal in the league and he was fully aware of the importance of the derby. "It doesn't matter if it's league or cup, it's always big and you have to win that one. Tottenham hadn't won at the Emirates. It was a great feeling to go there to win in my first derby, and especially to score. We played a bad first half, went 2-0 down, but in the second half we were a totally different team and that showed a lot of spirit."

Arsenal: Fabianski; Sagna, Koscielny, Squillaci, Clichy; Nasri (Walcott, 77), Fabregas, Denilson, Song, Arshavin (Rosicky, 77); Chamakh (van Persie, 68). Unused subs: Szczesny, Eboue, Wilshere, Djourou.

Spurs: Gomes; Hutton, Gallas, Kaboul, Assou-Ekotto; Lennon (Defoe, 46), Jenas, Modric, Bale; Van der Vaart (Palacios, 87); Pavlychenko (Crouch, 74). Unused subs: Cudicini, Bassong, Corluka, Bentley.

Goals: Arsenal - Nasri 9, Chamakh 27. Spurs - Bale 50, Van der Vaart 67 pen, Kaboul 85.

Attendance: 60,102.

Referee: Mr P Dowd.

ARSENAL
2 - 3
TOTTENHAM HOTSPUR
Autonomy

WHO AM I?

Can you identify the Spurs players below

Answers p58

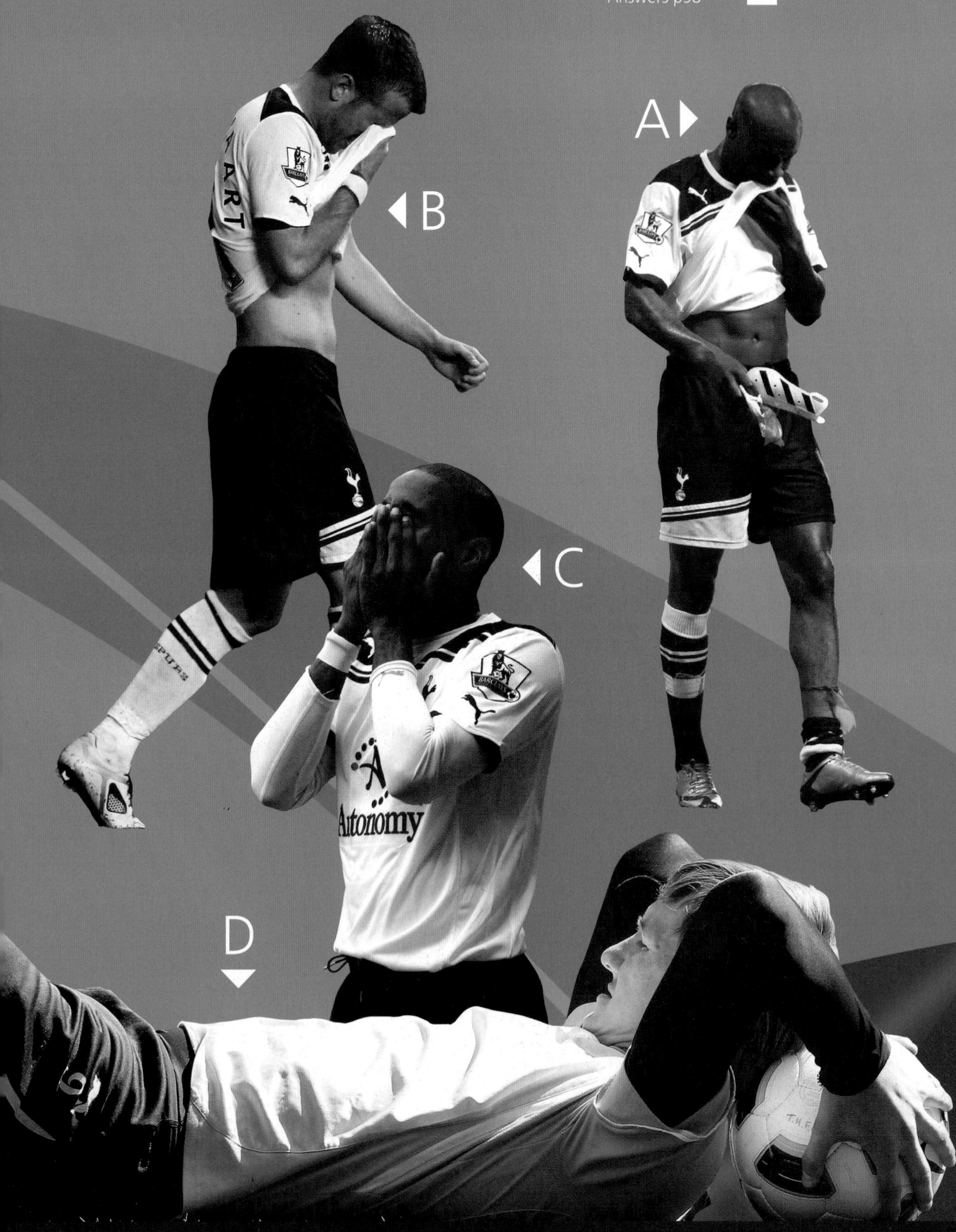

WORDSEARCH

Can you find the names of TEN Spurs players in this wordsearch? Words can go horizontally, vertically and diagonally.

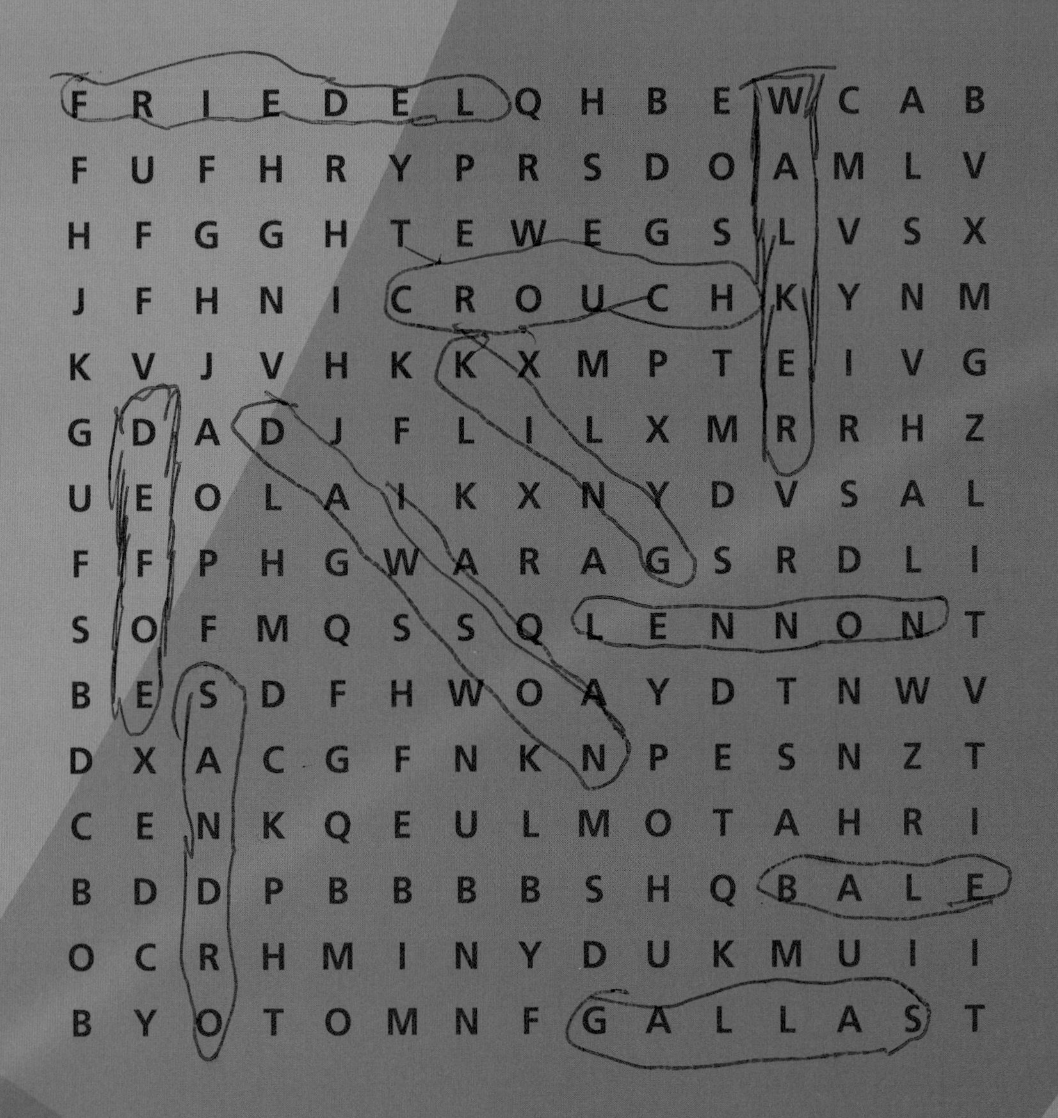

SANDRO DEFOE DAWSON GALLAS WALKER
BALE KING FRIEDEL LENNON CROUCH

Answers p58

Brad Friedel

Brad Friedel was our first summer signing after the American goalkeeper joined the club from Aston Villa. The 40-year-old turned down a host of high profile clubs to join Spurs. Brad signed a two-year contract at the end of last season.

Brad is now in another chapter in a long and successful career. Despite his age his natural fitness still makes him one the best goalkeepers in the Premier League. Friedel has a vast amount of Premier League experience, having moved to Liverpool in December 1997 from American side Columbus Crew. He only played 30 games for Liverpool before moving to Blackburn Rovers. His form at Blackburn made him a key part of a squad than won the League Cup against us in 2002. In total he made 356 appearances for Blackburn in eight successful years.

Brad joined Aston Villa in 2008 and his good form continued as they battled for European football under Martin O'Neill. In December he broke the record for consecutive top-flight appearances when he played in his 167th straight game - a run he had extended to 275 by the end of last season. Brad also enjoyed a long international career playing 82 games before retiring from international football in 2005, having represented his country at three World Cups.

Brad Friedel feels he's now part of one of the most talented squads of his distinguished career. "The squad that has been pulled together here is very, very talented, one of the most talented I've been a part of in football," said Brad. "I felt after speaking to the chairman and the manager that this was the place I wanted to be. "I liked the prospect of trying to help the team get back into the UEFA Champions League and I think the wealth of talent and the age of the players in the dressing room bodes well for Tottenham."

NEW SIGNINGS

Souleymane Coulibaly

Souleymane Coulibaly joined the Club in July 2011. The 16-year-old striker hit nine goals in four games for the Ivory Coast during the recent Under-17 World Cup - which included a hat-trick against Brazil and four against Denmark - to secure the golden boot and equal the tournament record set by former Liverpool striker Florent Sinama Pongolle, who achieved the milestone with three more games ten years ago. Souleymane had previously been part of the youth team of Italian side AC Siena.

Emmanuel Adebayor

Emmanuel Adebayor joined Spurs on a season-long loan from Manchester City. The Togo-born striker moved to the Premier League in January, 2006 from Monaco and has scored 81 goals in 186 appearances in all competitions during spells with Arsenal and Manchester City. Adebayor spent the second half of last season on loan at Real Madrid registering eight goals in 22 appearances.

FOOTBALL DEVELOPMENT

DIFFERENT CLASS

Courses available:
- Soccer Schools
- Roadshows
- The Spurs Academy Experience Coaching
- Premier Coaching Days
- Tottenham Hotspur Experience Days

TO BOOK, YOU CAN:
01: Visit tottenhamhotspur.com
02: Call 0208 365 5049

THE OFFICIAL MEMBERSHIP
ONE HOTSPUR

YOUNG AND GIFTED

WHEN YOU SIGN-UP A **ONE HOTSPUR JUNIOR** YOU'LL BE GIVING THEM A CONNECTION WITH SPURS THAT COULD LAST THEM A LIFETIME, PLUS SOME **EXCLUSIVE GOODIES** THAT YOU WON'T BE ABLE TO GET ANYWHERE ELSE!

TO JOIN OR GIVE MEMBERSHIP AS A GIFT, YOU CAN:
01: Visit tottenhamhotspur.com
02: Call 0208 365 5049
03: Visit the Ticket Office or Spurs Shops

10 Facts about TOTTENHAM HOTSPUR

We all know how great our club is but here are 10 facts about Spurs that make us a unique club in English football.

1. Following the formation of the Football League in 1888, Spurs became the first and only non-league team to lift the FA Cup in 1901.

2. Spurs were crowned Football League Champions and winners of the FA Cup in 1961. The first club to complete the 'Double' in the 20th century.

3. First British club to win a major European competition, winning the European Cup Winners Cup against Athletico Madrid in 1963.

4. Spurs were the first club to win the League Cup twice after defeating Norwich in the 1973 Final.

5. First English club to have played in three major European finals after our UEFA Cup match in 1974.

6. Spurs were the first football club to float shares on the London Stock Exchange in 1983.

7. In 1988 we made our first million plus signing Paul Stewart from Manchester City for £1.5 million.

8. Tottenham were the first club to lift the FA Cup with ribbons attached. Since 1901, the practice has been followed by every winning club since.

9. Aaron Lennon became the youngest Spurs player ever to play in the World Cup Finals after coming on as a substitute in England's match with Trinidad & Tobago. Aaron was 19 years and 60 days old.

10. In 2007 we celebrated our 125th anniversary.

UEFA Champions League Round of 16, 1st Leg

AC MILAN 0
TOTTENHAM HOTSPUR 1

Crouch (80)

Peter Crouch was the man once again to score the winner on another momentous night in the Club's history.

Investec

Fly Emirates
32

Investec
32
UEFA

SUPER SPURS QUIZ

It's a grand old team to play for and it's a grand old team to see, so if you know your history, try this 2012 Super Size Spurs Quiz.

1. Where did Spurs finish last season?

   5th

2. When did we first win the FA Cup?

   1900-01

3. Brad Friedel represented which nation?

   American

4. Name our matchday club mascot

   Chirphy

5. Name our opponents in Group A of last seasons UEFA Champions League

   inter milan, werder bremen, fc twent

6. Who was our top goalscorer last season?

   Van der vart

7. Who were our opponents in the 1961-62 Charity Shield?

8. Name the two clubs Kyle Walker was loaned to last season

9. True or false...Tottenham were the first British club to win a European trophy?

10. Who captained Spurs to the 2008 Carling Cup Final?

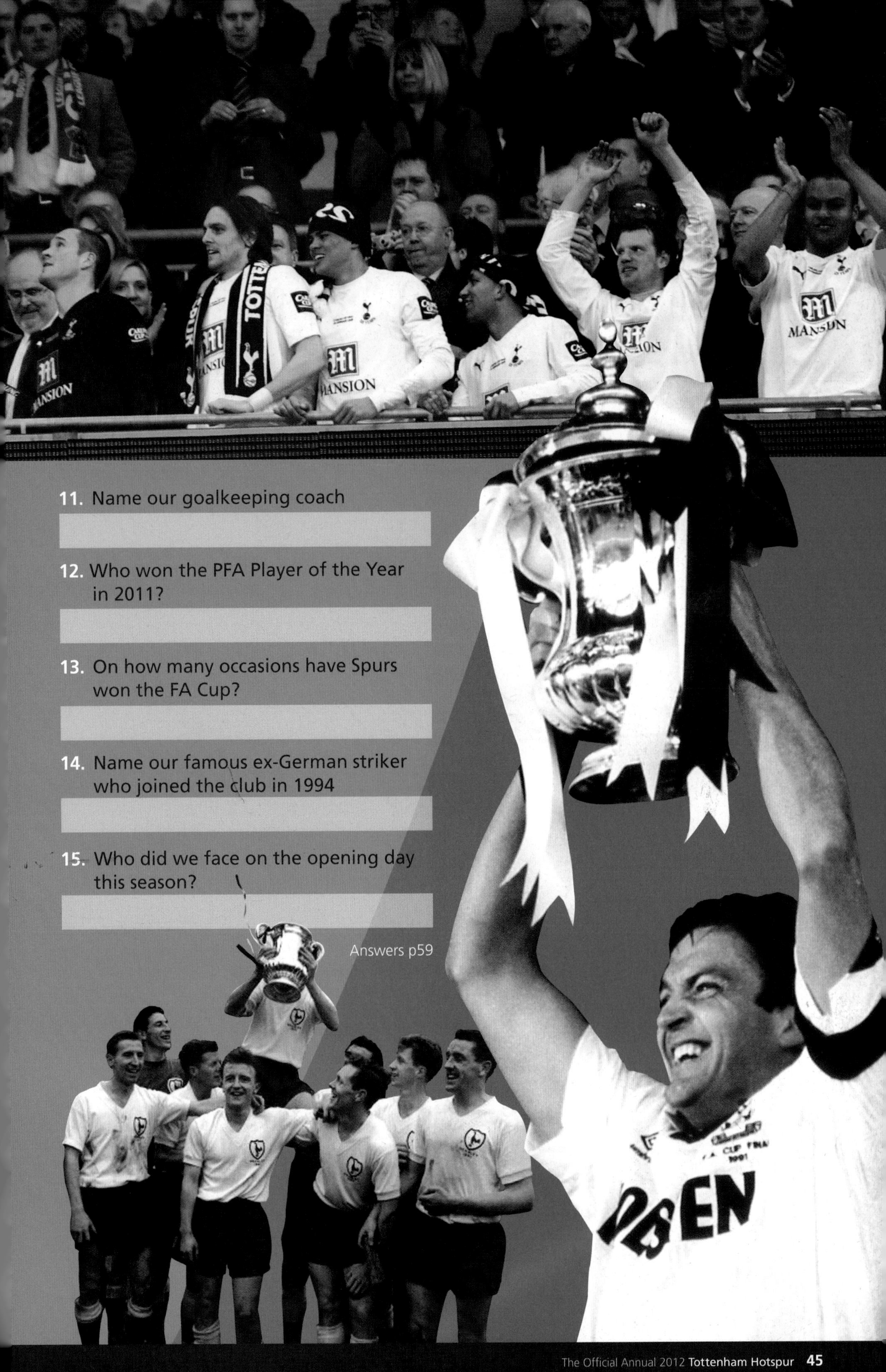

11. Name our goalkeeping coach

12. Who won the PFA Player of the Year in 2011?

13. On how many occasions have Spurs won the FA Cup?

14. Name our famous ex-German striker who joined the club in 1994

15. Who did we face on the opening day this season?

Answers p59

Kevin Bond

Kevin is now in his fourth season at the club after arriving in the same week Harry Redknapp joined Spurs from Portsmouth. He continues to play a vital role as our Assistant Manager.

Kevin started his football career as an apprentice at Bournemouth before returning for a second spell as a seasoned professional in 1988 and then managing the club between 2006-08.

Kevin played for Norwich, Manchester City and Southampton, racking up almost 400 appearances in the top flight and winning two England B caps in 1979-80. His playing career went full circle with a return to Bournemouth in 1988 - managed by none other than Harry Redknapp - and he made 126 league appearances before a short spell at Exeter.

Kevin followed in his father's footsteps by taking the managerial reins at Dean Court in 2006. Faced with a 10-point deduction, he almost kept the Cherries in League One in 2007-08. He then left to hook up again with Harry at Spurs.

Now into his fourth season at Spurs, Kevin is confident the club can have another memorable campaign. "We have steadily improved since Harry took over. To maintain and improve our position becomes more difficult each year but we'll thrive on the challenge. We have a good squad and I'm confident we can compete for major trophies."

Joe Jordan

Joe Jordan is a hugely valuable asset to Manager Harry Redknapp, joining Spurs shortly after Redknapp's arrival at the club.

Born in Carluke, Lanarkshire on December 15, 1951, Joe started his professional career with Greenock Morton aged 17 in 1968.

Joe joined Leeds United in 1970 and was soon representing Scotland. He played alongside the likes of Billy Bremner, Allan Clarke and Mick Jones in Don Revie's side. Joe picked up a European Cup Winners Cup Runners-Up medal after Leeds were beaten 1-0 by AC Milan in 1973. The following season Joe was part of the Leeds side that won the First Division title. Jordan spent three years at Manchester United where he scored 37 goals in 109 games. After Old Trafford, Joe moved to AC Milan scoring 12 goals in 52 games. After a brief spell at Verona Joe returned to England with Southampton, before ending his career as a player-manager at Bristol City.

RISING **STARS**

In a popular feature we profile four players who could set White Hart Lane alight in the future.

Steven Caulker

The England Under-21 central defender made his first team debut for the Club in September, 2010.

Coming off the back of an outstanding season-long loan at League One Yeovil Town in 2009-10, Steven returned from injury at the start of the following campaign to make his senior Spurs bow in our Carling Cup third round tie with Arsenal at the Lane.

After an impressive performance in the extra-time defeat, the 18-year-old made the step up to Championship level in joining Bristol City on loan for the remainder of the campaign.

Again he impressed, making 30 appearances, scoring twice, before a knee injury picked up in March ended the loan spell prematurely. Nonetheless, he picked up a Football League Young Player of the Month award and earned his first England Under-21 honours during his time at Ashton Gate.

Steven joined Premier League newcomers Swansea City on loan for the season to gain valuable top flight experience. Prior to his loan move, Caulker signed a new contract with Spurs.

Ryan Fredericks

The pacy right-winger signed a new contract with Tottenham in the summer. Ryan made it into the First Team squad for our FA Cup Fourth Round replay at Leeds United in 2010.

A winger who can play down the left or right side of midfield, he featured three times for our Under-18s in 2008-09 as an Under-16 player.

Thomas Carroll

Currently on loan at Leyton Orient, the midfielder got better and better throughout the 2009-10 campaign.

He ended with an impressive record of 10 goals in 21 appearances in the Premier Academy League, including 16 starts. He also started both FA Youth Cup ties.

In June, 2010, Tom signed his first professional contract at the Club and performed consistently for our Development Squad during the first half of the 2010-11 campaign before earning a loan move to Orient in January for the rest of the season.

Harry Kane

Manager Harry Redknapp was impressed with Harry Kane in the first week he was appointed Manager. Kane enjoyed a loan spell at League One side Leyton Orient last season. In season 2009-10 Harry scored 18 goals in 22 games for our Under-18s side.

His form earned him a place on the First Team bench on two occasions during the campaign, and he was rewarded his first professional contract at the Club in July, 2010.

Pre-Season Report

Spurs returned to South Africa for the Vodacom Challenge in pre-season. With a strong Spurs supporter base in the country it was a very worthwhile trip. We then returned to England as we prepared for another tough Premier League season.

KAIZER CHIEFS 1 SPURS 0

Kaizer Chiefs scored a dramatic late goal to win the first match of the Vodacom Challenge in Polokwane. George Lebese struck in the second of three minutes added time to send the home crowd into raptures at the Peter Mokaba Stadium.

ORLANDO PIRATES 1 SPURS 1

We were held to a 1-1 draw by South African champions Orlando Pirates in the second game of the 2011 Vodacom Challenge at the Mbombela Stadium, Nelspruit. Rafael van der Vaart opened the scoring with a superb free-kick before Happy Jele levelled for the Pirates.

ORLANDO PIRATES 0 SPURS 3

A 3-0 victory over Orlando Pirates at Coca-Cola Park, Johannesburg, gave us our first win of pre-season and the 2011 Vodacom Challenge title.

A Rafael van der Vaart double either side of half-time and Jermain Defoe's late strike made the scoreline look comfortable despite the South African champions missing a host of chances.

BRIGHTON 2 SPURS 3

We were proud and honoured to be chosen to officially open Brighton & Hove Albion's new American Express Community Stadium. Younes Kaboul , Vedran Corluka and Jake Livermore were on target for Spurs in a competitive friendly.

SPURS 2 ATHLETIC BILBAO 1

Our pre-season campaign was rounded off by a 2-1 win over an impressive Athletic Club Bilbao side. Trailing 1-0 at half-time, goals from Peter Crouch and Jermain Defoe secured victory.

SPOT THE **DIFFERENCE**

See if you can spot the 6 differences between the top and bottom pictures.

Answers p59

NEW **SIGNINGS**

Scott Parker

Scott Parker joined Spurs on transfer deadline day from West Ham. The England international's impressive displays for West Ham last season saw him named the Football Writers' Association Footballer of the Year.

The midfielder began his career with Charlton Athletic, making his debut in 1997 aged just 16, before joining Chelsea in January, 2004 and was crowned PFA Young Player of the Year at the end of the 2003/04 campaign.

Parker, who has represented England at every level from Under-16 through to senior, joined Newcastle United in June, 2005 and went on to captain the side during two seasons at St James' Park.

WHAT A **GOAL!!!**

We cannot remember a better season at Spurs for great goals. We re-live six amazing strikes from last season. Do you agree with our top six? Tweet @spursofficial and tell us your favourite goal!

GARETH BALE
STOKE 1
SPURS 2

Bale's second goal will long live in the memory. The lively Aaron Lennon again ran with the ball before arrowing a clever cross in the direction of Bale, who arched himself and dispatched a stunning left-foot volley into the top corner of the net.

GARETH BALE
INTER MILAN 4
SPURS 3

In a memorable game, Bale picked up a loose ball inside his own half and made a trademark gallop into Inter's box, leaving a trail of blue and black shirts in his wake, before drilling low and hard into the far corner. Gareth went on to score two more fantastic goals.

ROMAN PAVLYUCHENKO
BOLTON 4
SPURS 2

Roman scored some superb goals last season but his stunning volley from the angle at Bolton was arguably his most impressive.

RAFAEL van der VAART

ASTON VILLA 1 SPURS 2

The move started with a lung-busting run on the counter from Gareth Bale. The brilliant wide man cut inside and unselfishly tried to play in Lennon, who had other ideas. After checking, Lennon picked out van der Vaart who steered his second of the evening into the bottom corner.

NIKO KRANJCAR

SPURS 2 BOLTON 1

It looked like both teams would be settling for a point before, suddenly, Lennon found space to run, played inside to Pavlyuchenko who teed it up for Niko Kranjcar to side-step his marker and fire into the top corner with his left foot.

SANDRO

CHELSEA 2 SPURS 1

On 19 minutes a long Bale throw to Rafael van der Vaart was dinked in the direction of the on-rushing Sandro, who proceeded to arrow an unstoppable shot beyond Petr Cech and into the top corner of the net.

Domestic Cups Review

Our participation in the FA Cup and Carling Cup both came to a premature end last season.

FA CUP THIRD ROUND

TOTTENHAM HOTSPUR 3-0 CHARLTON ATHLETIC

A packed White Hart Lane crowd saw Andros Townsend score his first professional goal for the club as we beat League One Charlton. The first half proved to be frustrating, with Charlton defending well but a goal from Townsend and a quick double from Jermain Defoe, earned us a place in the fourth round.

Spurs (4-4-2): Cudicini; Corluka, Bassong, Dawson, Assou-Ekotto; Townsend, Palacios (Modric 46), Sandro, Kranjcar; Defoe, Pavlyuchenko.

FA CUP FOURTH ROUND

FULHAM 4-0 TOTTENHAM HOTSPUR

Our Fourth Round trip to Craven Cottage was a game to forget. Fulham went ahead from the penalty spot after Alan Hutton brought down Clint Dempsey. The tie was all but over when Michael Dawson was sent off for his foul on Moussa Dembele. Danny Murphy scored both penalties. Brede Hangeland made it 3-0 and Dembele scored before half-time to seal a forgettable encounter.

Spurs: Gomes; Hutton, Bassong, Dawson, Assou-Ekotto; Van der Vaart (Jenas, 67), Modric, Sandro (Gallas, 12), Pienaar, Lennon; Defoe (Crouch, 46).

CARLING CUP THIRD ROUND

TOTTENHAM HOTSPUR 1-4 ARSENAL

With Champions League and Premier League matches coming thick and fast, Harry Redknapp decided to make a host of changes. Goalkeeper Stipe Pletikosa, young defender Steven Caulker and summer recruit Sandro all came in for their debuts, while Jake Livermore made his first start and Kyle Naughton only his second. Sebastien Bassong was named captain. Arsenal fielded a near full strength side which surprised many, as Arsène Wenger looked to seal a first trophy for the club since 2005. Henri Lansbury gave the Gunners the lead before Robbie Keane levelled in the second half. Two Samir Nasri penalties in extra-time and another from Andrey Arshavin signalled our exit from the Carling Cup.

Spurs: Pletikosa; Naughton, Caulker, Bassong, Assou-Ekotto; Palacios, Livermore (Lennon, 46), Sandro (Kranjcar, 96), Bentley; Giovani (Keane, 46); Pavlyuchenko.

13

Investec
Investec

krbs
macron
32

QUIZ ANSWERS

How did you get on this year?

WHO AM I? p36

A	WILLIAM GALLAS
B	RAFAEL VAN DER VAART
C	JERMAIN DEFOE
D	ROMAN PAVLYUCHENKO

WORDSEARCH p37

F	R	I	E	D	E	L	Q	H	B	E	W	C	A	B
F	U	F	H	R	Y	P	R	S	D	O	A	M	L	V
H	F	G	G	H	T	E	W	E	G	S	L	V	S	X
J	F	H	N	I	C	R	O	U	C	H	K	Y	N	M
K	V	J	V	H	K	K	X	M	P	T	E	I	V	G
G	D	A	D	J	F	L	I	L	X	M	R	R	H	Z
U	E	O	L	A	I	K	X	N	Y	D	V	S	A	L
F	F	P	H	G	W	A	R	A	G	S	R	D	L	I
S	O	F	M	Q	S	S	Q	L	E	N	N	O	N	T
B	E	S	D	F	H	W	O	A	Y	D	T	N	W	V
D	X	A	C	G	F	N	K	N	P	E	S	N	Z	T
C	E	N	K	Q	E	U	L	M	O	T	A	H	R	I
B	D	D	P	B	B	B	B	S	H	Q	B	A	L	E
O	C	R	H	M	I	N	Y	D	U	K	M	U	I	I
B	Y	O	T	O	M	N	F	G	A	L	L	A	S	T

SUPER SPURS QUIZ p44-45

1 5th
2 1901
3 United States
4 Chirpy
5 Inter Milan, Werder Bremen & FC Twente
6 Rafael van der Vaart
7 England Select XI
8 QPR & Aston Villa
9 True
10 Ledley King
11 Tony Parks
12 Gareth Bale
13 Eight
14 Jurgen Klinsmann
15 Everton

How did you do?

15-15 = The ultimate Spurs supporter
11-14 = Impressive, make sure you get all 15 in the 2013 Annual!
7-10 = Mid-table finish
1-6 = Do you support Arsenal?

SPOT THE DIFFERENCE p52

RESULTS, TROPHIES & STATS

Major Honours

Football League Champions:	**1950-51, 1960-61**
F.A.Cup Winners:	**1900-01, 1920-21, 1960-61, 1961-62, 1966-67, 1980-81, 1981-82, 1990-91**
Football League Cup Winners:	**1970-71, 1972-73, 1998-99, 2007-08**
European Cup-Winners Cup Winners:	**1962-63**
UEFA Cup Winners:	**1971-72, 1983-84**
F.A.Charity Shield Winners:	**1920-21, 1951-52, 1961-62, 1962-63, 1967-68 (joint), 1981-82 (joint), 1991-92 (joint).**

Results 2010-11

AUGUST 2010				H	A	
14 Sat	Home	Man City	Barclays Premier League	0	0	35,928
17 Tue	Away	BSC Young Boys	UEFA Champions League	2	3	30,166
21 Sat	Away	Stoke City	Barclays Premier League	2	1	27,243
25 Wed	Home	BSC Young Boys	UEFA Champions League	4	0	34,709
28 Sat	Home	Wigan Athletic	Barclays Premier League	0	1	35,101
SEPTEMBER 2010				H	A	
11 Sat	Away	West Brom	Barclays Premier League	1	1	23,642
14 Tue	Away	Werder Bremen	UEFA Champions League	2	2	30,344
18 Sat	Home	Wolves	Barclays Premier League	3	1	35,940
21 Tue	Home	Arsenal	Carling Cup	1	4	35,883
25 Sat	Away	West Ham	Barclays Premier League	0	1	34,190
29 Wed	Home	FC Twente	UEFA Champions League	4	1	32,318
OCTOBER 2010				H	A	
02 Sat	Home	Aston Villa	Barclays Premier League	2	1	35,871
16 Sat	Away	Fulham	Barclays Premier League	2	1	25,615
20 Wed	Away	Inter Milan	UEFA Champions League	3	4	49,551
23 Sat	Home	Everton	Barclays Premier League	1	1	N/A
30 Sat	Away	Man Utd	Barclays Premier League	0	2	75,223
NOVEMBER 2010				H	A	
02 Tue	Home	Inter Milan	UEFA Champions League	3	1	N/A
06 Sat	Away	Bolton	Barclays Premier League	2	4	20,225
09 Tue	Home	Sunderland	Barclays Premier League	1	1	35,843
13 Sat	Home	Blackburn	Barclays Premier League	4	2	35,700
20 Sat	Away	Arsenal	Barclays Premier League	3	2	60,102
24 Wed	Home	Werder Bremen	UEFA Champions League	3	0	33,546
28 Sun	Home	Liverpool	Barclays Premier League	2	1	35,692
DECEMBER 2010				H	A	
04 Sat	Away	Birmingham	Barclays Premier League	1	1	25,770
07 Tue	Away	FC Twente	UEFA Champions League	3	3	24,000
12 Sun	Home	Chelsea	Barclays Premier League	1	1	35,787
26 Sun	Away	Aston Villa	Barclays Premier League	2	1	39,411
28 Tue	Home	Newcastle Utd	Barclays Premier League	2	0	35,927
JANUARY 2011				H	A	
01 Sat	Home	Fulham	Barclays Premier League	1	0	35,603
05 Wed	Away	Everton	Barclays Premier League	1	2	34,124
09 Sun	Home	Charlton Athletic	The FA Cup	3	0	35,698
16 Sun	Home	Man Utd	Barclays Premier League	0	0	35,828
22 Sat	Away	Newcastle Utd	Barclays Premier League	1	1	51,010
30 Sun	Away	Fulham	The FA Cup	0	4	21,829

FEBRUARY 2011				H	A	
02 Wed	Away	Blackburn	Barclays Premier League	1	0	23,253
05 Sat	Home	Bolton	Barclays Premier League	2	1	36,197
12 Sat	Away	Sunderland	Barclays Premier League	2	1	40,986
15 Tue	Away	AC Milan	UEFA Champions League	1	0	75,652
22 Tue	Away	Blackpool	Barclays Premier League	1	3	16,069
MARCH 2011				H	A	
06 Sun	Away	Wolves	Barclays Premier League	3	3	28,669
09 Wed	Home	AC Milan	UEFA Champions League	0	0	34,320
19 Sat	Home	West Ham	Barclays Premier League	0	0	36,010
APRIL 2011				H	A	
02 Sat	Away	Wigan Athletic	Barclays Premier League	0	0	18,578
05 Tue	Away	Real Madrid	UEFA Champions League	0	4	71,657
09 Sat	Home	Stoke City	Barclays Premier League	3	2	35,702
13 Wed	Home	Real Madrid	UEFA Champions League	0	1	34,311
20 Wed	Home	Arsenal	Barclays Premier League	3	3	36,138
23 Sat	Home	West Brom	Barclays Premier League	2	2	36,160
30 Sat	Away	Chelsea	Barclays Premier League	1	2	41,681
MAY 2011				H	A	
07 Sat	Home	Blackpool	Barclays Premier League	1	1	35,585
10 Tue	Away	Man City	Barclays Premier League	0	1	47,069
15 Sun	Away	Liverpool	Barclays Premier League	2	0	44,893
22 Sun	Home	Birmingham	Barclays Premier League	2	1	36,119

2010-11 Player Appearances

PLAYER	LEAGUE APPS / GLS		FA CUP APPS / GLS		LEAGUE CUP APPS / GLS		EUROPE APPS / GLS	
Ben Alnwick (G)	0 (0)	0	0 (0)	0	0 (0)	0	0 (0)	0
Benoit Assou-Ekotto (D)	30 (0)	0	2 (0)	0	1 (0)	0	12 (0)	0
Gareth Bale (M)	29 (1)	7	0 (0)	0	0 (0)	0	10 (1)	4
Sebastien Bassong (D)	7 (5)	1	2 (0)	0	1 (0)	0	4 (1)	1
David Bentley (M)	1 (1)	0	0 (0)	0	1 (0)	0	0 (0)	0
John Bostock (M)	0 (0)	0	0 (0)	0	0 (0)	0	0 (0)	0
Steven Caulker (D)	0 (0)	0	0 (0)	0	1 (0)	0	0 (0)	0
Vedran Corluka (D)	13 (2)	0	1 (0)	0	0 (0)	0	8 (0)	0
Peter Crouch (F)	20 (14)	4	0 (1)	0	0 (0)	0	9 (1)	7
Carlo Cudicini (G)	8 (0)	0	1 (0)	0	0 (0)	0	2 (2)	0
Michael Dawson (D)	24 (0)	1	2 (0)	0	0 (0)	0	6 (0)	0
Jermain Defoe (F)	16 (6)	4	2 (0)	2	0 (0)	0	3 (3)	3
Giovani Dos Santos (M)	0 (3)	0	0 (0)	0	1 (0)	0	1 (0)	0
William Gallas (D)	26 (1)	0	0 (1)	0	0 (0)	0	8 (0)	0
Heurelho Gomes (G)	30 (0)	0	1 (0)	0	0 (0)	0	10 (0)	0
Tom Huddlestone (M)	13 (1)	2	0 (0)	0	0 (0)	0	6 (1)	0
Alan Hutton (D)	19 (2)	2	1 (0)	0	0 (0)	0	4 (0)	0
Jermaine Jenas (M)	14 (5)	0	0 (1)	0	0 (0)	0	5 (3)	0
Younes Kaboul (D)	19 (2)	1	0 (0)	0	0 (0)	0	3 (0)	1
Robbie Keane (F)	2 (5)	0	0 (0)	0	0 (1)	1	0 (5)	0
Bongani Khumalo (D)	0 (0)	0	0 (0)	0	0 (0)	0	0 (0)	0
Ledley King (D)	(0)	0	0 (0)	0	0 (0)	0	3 (0)	0
Niko Kranjcar (M)	2 (11)	2	1 (0)	0	0 (1)	0	1 (5)	0
Aaron Lennon (M)	25 (9)	3	1 (0)	0	0 (1)	0	8 (2)	0
Jake Livermore (M)	0 (0)	0	0 (0)	0	1 (0)	0	0 (0)	0
Luka Modric (M)	32 (0)	3	1 (1)	0	0 (0)	0	8 (1)	1
Kyle Naughton (D)	0 (0)	0	0 (0)	0	1 (0)	0	0 (0)	0
Wilson Palacios (M)	16 (5)	0	1 (0)	0	1 (0)	0	4 (4)	0
Roman Pavlyuchenko (F)	18 (11)	10	1 (0)	0	1 (0)	0	5 (3)	4
Steven Pienaar (M)	5 (3)	0	1 (0)	0	0 (0)	0	2 (0)	0
Stipe Pletikosa (G)	0 (0)	0	0 (0)	0	1 (0)	0	0 (0)	0
Danny Rose (M)	4 (0)	0	0 (0)	0	0 (0)	0	0 (0)	0
Sandro (M)	11 (8)	1	2 (0)	0	1 (0)	0	3 (1)	0
Andros Townsend (M)	0 (0)	0	1 (0)	1	0 (0)	0	0 (0)	0
Kyle Walker (D)	0 (1)	0	0 (0)	0	0 (0)	0	0 (0)	0
Jonathan Woodgate (D)	0 (0)	0	0 (0)	0	0 (0)	0	0 (1)	0
Rafael van der Vaart (M)	28 (0)	13	1 (0)	0	0 (0)	0	7 (0)	2

WHERE'S CHIRPY?
Autonomy
Autonomy
Autonomy
MANSION
COPA